Naked Me

An Assortment of Reflections

Fay Campbell

For

my very cool mother,

LaVon Dozina Shubert Campbell,

who never doubted I could do it.

I love you!

www.FayCampbell.com

CAMPIAN BELLSTONE PUBLISHERS
Richmond, Virginia, USA
www.BellstoneBooks.com

Naked Me: An Assortment of Reflections
by Fay Campbell
Edited and designed by Ian F. Wesley
ISBN 978-1-940670-01-0

1. Poetry   2. Ballads
3. Short Fiction   4. Lyrics
5. Nature

Photography by Fay Campbell
Royal Oak credit: Brian Chislett

This book is available in
paperback and e-book editions

Contents

SECTION IV: TESTOSTERONE

Acknowledgments

I am blessed to have always been surrounded by strong women. At a time when single, educated women were a bit rare, my childhood neighborhood was full of them. Dr. Kibbe and Dr. Jones were professors of biology and literature at Carthage College. Dorothy and Virginia Frazee, next door, had degrees in music and microbiology. They all nurtured my love of Nature, music and words from a very young age.

Virginia Allison taught me that one has to know the rules of writing in order to successfully break them. And I think of her every time I start a sentence with a conjunction, I apologize for any comma splices now.

My sister, Nancy, and my daughter, Devin, are possibly the strongest and smartest women I know, so when they said, "You've got to publish this!" I figured it must be a good idea.

James and my son, Patrick, taught me by example how to live a dream.

Valerie, thanks for always supporting me even though you don't like poetry.

Ian Wesley, my agentpublisherfriend, thanks so much for fathering this baby.

Foreword

Why *Naked Me?*
No, there are no pictures of me in the buff in this book. However, writing honest fiction and poetry for others to read feels very much like dancing across the stage neked as a jay bird. It is possibly the bravest thing I've ever done.

I'm a listener. It doesn't seem to matter what my job title is—and I've had more than a few—people with whom I interact always seem to see a tattoo on my forehead that reads:

Please Tell Me Your Stories!

And they do.

However, not one of these stories has actually been told to me *as such*. I don't divulge secrets. I think that's a nasty thing to do, and besides, I can't remember them anyway. But, what I have gleaned is a whole paint box full of possibilities for stories, for snippets of life that have fed my imagination, and which I've arranged and rearranged. In the "Testosterone" section, I have created women who talk very openly about their exploits, sometimes in poetry or song and sometimes in prose.

"Fearless" is just the way we ought to live, don't you think? This first section is a collection of stories about the fears and silliness all people face. Here I tell some things that I think are important enough to say about the human condition. A couple of pub songs were inspired by a visit to Southwest England, a place I love.

I've always been blessed with detailed, elaborate dreams. I am a lucid dreamer and harvest abundantly from the ethers. The pieces in the section "Dream Play" were inspired by some of those glimpses into that other world.

"Au Naturel" celebrates an ongoing love affair with Nature. I am grateful with every breath that I was raised to appreciate all of Earth. I will sing the lullaby, "Such Big Love," to my darling grandson, Bump.

SECTION I

Fearless

USS *Arizona*

September 11, 2001, changed everything. What changed within me was that I became fearless.

I decided to take up an old friend's offer and go to Hawaii for about 10 days. It wasn't a trip I could really afford, but somehow that didn't scare me. After the attacks, my friend had been called back to the Navy to do something technical and secret. He arranged for me to stay in a room in bachelor officers' quarters on base. He worked at night and gave me use of his car, which, of course, had the appropriate tags, and I learned to salute back at the very young sailors who let me and the car on base.

I was staying at Pearl Harbor over Pearl Harbor Day, just after the 2001 attacks on the Twin Towers. I thought that I might be afraid. But once there, I realized I was in one of the most protected places on Earth—Hickam Air Force Base and Pearl Harbor Naval Base with me smack dab in the middle. I was safe. (Well, safe from enemy attacks. But the place was crawling—rather, strutting—with young naval officers in white dress uniforms. Lord, have mercy! Who designs those uniforms? My, my, my! But I digress.)

My friend said, "You can't get too lost. We're on an island. Find the ocean and just keep driving and you'll find your way back to base." And he was right. It was a grand adventure. I drove around that island like I knew what I was doing. The ocean was unbelievable colors. Surfers defied gravity. I soaked up sun and floated on the Pacific, hardly able to believe how beautiful it all was and that I was enjoying it mostly alone. I went through the markets and bought sarongs, which I wore! I ate strange things. I bought strange things. I talked to strangers.

I decided to do the tour of the USS Arizona, though I can't say I was really looking forward to it. What I like best about military stuff is those uniforms. I sat through the short video and learned a bunch of information about the 1941 attack on Pearl Harbor that I didn't know. It was, after all, before my time.

Then a group of visitors, Americans, Japanese, old and young, took a ferry across the water to the monument built directly over the sunken ship. The ferry stopped and the captain asked us to stay where we were until an American survivor of the attack had disembarked.

A very old, very proud, very tearful man in a wheel chair was pushed up the aisle past us, and, row by row, we silently stood in his honor. When he got to the ramp, he insisted on walking. Two young sailors helped him to his feet and aided him as he walked onto the monument.

We all cried that day. Tears of loss, tears of reconciliation, tears of disbelief, and, I think, of healing.

It was fitting, I think, that looking down into the water above the USS Arizona, I saw rainbows of oil slicks from fuel still slowly leaking from the tomb and a perfect sky reflected in the harbor, now bit deeper from so many tears.

ABCs

I have 58 years. I have two grown children and a perfect grandson. I've had so dang many great adventures; I can't count them all. I know how ridiculous mothers can be—I *are* one. I know the panic of hearing my mother's words come right out of my mouth when my children were young. I recall them laughing at me when I tried to catch the words out of the air and stuff them back down my pie hole. Now, when my mother's words come out of my mouth, I want to claim them as my own. The older I got, the cooler and wiser my mother became. You can imagine how cool and wise she is now, at age 90. Go figure.

I know I can tell my beloved children things and share what I've learned with them. I also know I have nothing to say about if and when they hear it. Yet most of the time, there's something that compels me to tell them anyway.

I'm going to try to distill some things I want them to hear, knowing I'm not even going to scratch the surface.

A Let Love and gentleness be your default setting.
Anger and negativity incite anger and negativity.
Love and positivity incite Love and positivity.
If you want to stop an argument, stop arguing.
If someone is pushing something at you, give
them nothing to push against. And for crying in

4

a bucket, be loving and gentle with yourselves. You can't give what you do not have.

B Play. Create. Be silly. Laugh at yourself. Frolic. Dance every chance you get.

C Realize the only boundaries are those that you imagine. This is not just some cutesy saying. It's quantum physics, by golly! You are Nature and Nature is you, and that is so very wonderful. Please love trees. Some of my best friends have been trees. When you are off-kilter, take off your shoes and get your feet in the dirt and hold on to a friendly tree. You will be connected to Heaven and Earth.

D Know that if you are breathing you have everything you need.

E Grasp the truth that material wealth is diddly squat in the overall picture. Check out that big picture regularly. It will keep you humble.

F Garden.

G Realize that at the end of your life you probably won't regret things you've done as much as things you haven't. Don't be afraid to strike every single match in your box. The box won't get empty, though unused matches may get soggy and lose their ability to bring fire.

H Be fearless. Absolutely fearless. Ask yourself what you'd do if you knew you could not fail, then go flippin' do it.

I Know that the truth is the truth, even if no one believes it, and a lie is a lie, even if everyone believes it. Stand for what you know is right, with bravery, gentleness, determination, and respect.

J Never let anyone else think for you. Never let anyone, anything or any organization, institution, or government convince you to abdicate thinking.

K Admit when you've been wrong and apologize.

L Just know that into every life some shit will hit the fan. It is just gonna happen. You'll be hurt, and your heart will be broken. My bridge master used to say, "If you aren't going set a third of the time, you're being a sissy." Don't be a sissy. So you get some scars. How boring to have none.

M Don't waste—not resources, not talent, not energy, not a starry night, not a sunny day, nor a good night's sleep dreaming. Avoid vampires.

N Be grateful. You are blessed. Be grateful first and last.

O Choose to be happy.

P It's never too late to change, grow, learn, improve.

Q Know it's not up to you to fix everything.

R Never stop learning. Never stop seeking knowledge.

S You have wings. You have roots.

T Keep the few great friends very close to your heart.

U Remember the law of Karma. Do good things for others daily.

V Forgive quickly. Love freely. Kiss your mate slowly, daily.

W Share everything, especially what you've learned. If no one listens, no worries.

X Learn to accept a gift with grace. All that you are and everything that you have are gifts.

Y Know this too shall pass.

Z And try to understand that although you didn't have perfect parents, you have parents who love you completely, without hesitation or exception. Yeah, we are pretty cool people.

She Still Chooses

She chose those—
    Those clothes, those shows, those beaux,
Heaven knows,
    She didn't do without beaux.

Now, nearer
    The close than the beginning,
She remembers
    Losing more than winning,
        Never looked at it as sinning,
            Knew there'd always be more innings,
                And she always left them grinning.

And it looks as if it's true,
Though she really never knew,
If one could really live as two,
And be happy as they do
Together their whole lives through.

What is it that she hadn't done
While laughing fast toward the sun?
She often thought she'd found the one,
But soon as it had begun,
She called it done.

She could not let another in,
She'd never lose, and never win.
So left alone in silent din,
Too tired to begin again,
She fixes photos with a pin.

She takes her memories one by one
And watches them fade in the sun,
Too tired and too wise to run,
And satisfied with all the fun,
She wonders if it's all now done.

A tap upon the rusted gate!
Might there be such thing as fate?
Perhaps it isn't all too late?
Perhaps there is someone who'll wait,
While her internal storms abate?

The storm now blows with much less fury
And she's in much less a hurry.
And older vision, clearly blurry,
Sees it's truth, is judge and jury,
Knows there's no answer to life's query.

Why not once more! What's there to lose?
Maybe together, but not fused,
Not so close that they might bruise,
Not for answers, just for clues,
Always more for them to choose.

Spinning

Around your life, so tightly wound,
The thread you spin of what is left of you
Keeps everything and everyone in place—
    Exactly the correct place.
No room for mistakes or tears.
Too many rely on your perfection.

When will it be your time—
The time for the thread you spin
    To create something just for you?
Perhaps a shawl to keep out the cold
And on which to dry your tears?

Blanche

A long weekend yawns ahead.
My old dog snores beside me on the bed.
She dreams of pain-free days of jumping high.
Hearing sharp and clear brown eyes.

Her white muzzle twitches in a smile.
I let her sleep to run another mile.
Paws hint of hopping through the grass,
Dreaming of puppy days long past.

Independence

When I can't remember, will you remember me?
Who will lead me on, when my eyes no longer see?
Who will speak for me when my words are gone?
When I cannot sing, who will know my song?

When I am lost, who will take my hand?
When I am weak, who will help me stand?
Independence ransoms itself—
There is no intrinsic warmth in only wealth.

Broken Things

I was two when we moved next door to Mrs. Frazee. Right away I made a great friend. Mrs. Frazee was wonderful. She had the longest hair in the world, which she brushed out early in the morning and then braided and wound into a bun on her head. She read to me and told me stories and gave me many, many gifts.

She told me the story of pansies. I can't remember it completely, and I've tried to locate it in a book with no success. Perhaps she made up that story just for me. It had to do with a queen and her handmaidens. I think of her whenever I see pansies.

Once, when I was around four, she gave me a beautiful china lady. I think it was from Germany. It was someplace far away. Mrs. Frazee never treated me like a clumsy, little kid. She let me carry my treasure home by myself. It was so precious, so delicate. I felt very big.

Then the terrible thing happened. I dropped that precious china lady. The delicate present and my heart were shattered. My mother came out of nowhere, the way mothers do, and gathered me and the pieces of china. She set about to glue the lady together and Mrs. Frazee set about fixing me.

My dear friend told me that the accident could be just our secret. No one else needed to know. She also let me know that sometimes things break. That's just the way things are. It isn't the end of the world or the end

13

of a friendship. It doesn't have to be the end of trust. It's not the end of love. She taught me not to be afraid of carrying my gifts home, and that was probably the biggest gift of all.

Mrs. Frazee gave me lots of gifts. I have a mirror and hair brush that look like tortoise shell. I have a perfume bottle that is a hundred different colors. I have an adult-sized tea set, lots of stories, and some secrets. I also have a glued pink china lady.

I imagine that an antique dealer might find my china lady valuable if it hadn't been shattered long ago by a little girl. It is priceless to me, at least in part, because it was.

Give the Girl a Hand

She smiles.
She lies.
It is a part she plays well.
Give the girl a hand!

What a performance!
Stand and applaud,
Call for an encore!
She plays for the one person in his seat.

She will try harder,
Sing louder, dance faster,
Until she slips on her tears and sweat,
Proving that she was never good enough.

The mask has grown into her skin.
Beneath the wig her head is shaved.
She can't find her way off the stage.
Give the girl a hand.

Christmas

A season apart

Nods to silent, holy nights

Forgotten in the din.

My Eyes Are Sore from Crying

My eyes are sore from crying,
And I just want to smile.
No string, no expectations,
Just hold me for a while.

I won't ask you for the morning—
No tomorrows, no next years.
Let's both forget the details;
Come and hold me near.

Once I Loved an Englishman

Once I loved an Englishman,
An Englishman, he were.
I sometimes thought he loved me back
And there were no other her.
But when I said, "I love you, John,"
He'd tug down on his hat,
And give me such a sly wee wink,
Say'n, "We'll speak no more o' that."

Once I loved an Irishman,
An Irishman, he were,
I sometimes thought he loved me back
And there were no other her.
But when I said, "I love ya, Pat,"
He'd look me in the eye,
And say, "My Dear, please fill my glass,
My throat's becomin' dry."

Once I loved a Scottish man
A Scotsman, that he were.
I sometimes thought he loved me back
And there were no other her.
But when I said, "I love you, Mac,"
And my eyes would fill with tears,
He'd look me 'round and squeeze me arm,
'N ask, "How fast can ye shear?"

So I spoke no more about it,
Poured beer in Paddy's glass,
And I built myself up tough 'n strong,
And became a sturdy lass.
I did what each one wanted,
Bein' never one to fail.
Then pa said, "Now you're a right good catch."
And sent me off to Wales.

CLEVEDON, ENGLAND

Pour me another pint of cider,
Sweet elixir from the tree.
God knows, there's nothing wrong with apples,
And cider's very good for me.

Pour me another pint of cider,
Shiny, warming, liquid gold.
Happy, hardy rounds of laughter
Ring with every story told.

Pour me another pint of cider,
Wholesome sunshine from a glass.
And don't dare say I've had too many,
'Till I fall down on my ass.

SECTION II

Dream Play

Reflections in a Pond

I saw a little girl about my age, carrying a basket past the house. The basket looked full of large, brown onions, but maybe they were kittens. I skipped along beside her for a while, and she didn't notice me. I didn't mind. I ran barefoot back to the house through the new snow. The frozen twigs on the trees on the sides of the house stung my cheeks. I rounded the corner to the porch—the side of the house in the sun—where there was just a little snow left.

I climbed up the steps to the door. The last step was missing, and I stopped to study the partially-opened door. The paint was peeling off in big flakes—yellow green on the outside and darker green on the underside. Beneath the green layer was brown and grey. It looked a bit like leaves on a tree in early autumn. I climbed inside to the kitchen.

I said, "Mama, look! I can see right through the floor!"

She said, "I don't reckon you'll fall through before Pa gets back," but she didn't look at me when she said it. She was looking at her broom.

The house had been alone too long. Not alone, exactly, but without people. The animals liked the holes in the floor and walls. Little Man was living there when we arrived and he adopted us—a giant of a dog, fiercely protective of us, but afraid to drink from a water bowl. Mama said he was crazy.

Pa carved things out of fallen trees and branches, and he had a hand cart that he filled with them and pushed away to somewhere. If we were lucky, when he came back, he had flour and salt, clothes, and stuff Mama needed. Today we were hoping for a blanket.

"Can't put good carvin' wood in the stove," said Mama as I was thinking about doing just that. Not that it made a lot of difference with all the holes in the house, but it sure would have been nice to warm my wet feet.

When Pa got back it was near dark. He had lots of treasures, including three blankets! One was just for me. As I was going to sleep, I heard Mama say something about us maybe getting squatting rights, but I wasn't sure what that meant. She was crying. I wished she would just stop.

Time was funny then. It seemed by morning the house was healed a bit. There weren't holes in the floor anymore, though it still sloped. And the door was different. The big leafy flakes weren't there anymore, but it was okay. I could still see bits of all the colors. They were just smoothed out now.

I figured out how to shimmy up the tall tree by the pond. I'd sort of reach around it, like I was hugging it up as high as I could, pull myself up, then sort of grab with my feet up high as I could and kept pulling and pushing myself up that way until I reached the only fork in the tree. I don't know what sort of tree this was. He was tall, only about eight inches across, and only the one fork, and it was far up. I guess it had to grow like that, sort of squeezing in among the shadows of bigger trees so as to get his share of sunlight. Clever tree.

I loved shimmying up that tree for three reasons. *One:* I figured out how to do it all by myself, which is usually the way I figured things out, but this was the best one. *Two:* when I was up there, no one saw me. It wasn't because they couldn't see me, it's just that people—most people—forget to look up. I reckon most people go around seeing only a little part of what's there because they forget to look up, and they forget to get right down on the ground and look down. Little Man and I are the exceptions. We both look up so often we trip over things and then we end up looking at the ground real close up. Ha! *Three:* I could hear all sorts of conversations that weren't meant for me, when I was up there. Not just Mama and Pa, but birds and squirrels, too. I just loved the trust we had, that tree and me.

Once I got to the fork, I'd sort of weave myself with the two branches, and then I could just be still. The wind would move the tree slowly back and forth, like I think most mamas rock their babies. The tree's smooth bark covered such hard wood. It was a strong, gentle tree, and it held me quietly and safely and Little Man took naps at his base. I was so safe.

Oh, and there's a number four, too! From up the tree, I could see very far away. I could see houses that weren't there when I was on the ground. Sometimes, I could see people that went with the houses, not that far from us. I could hear them sometimes, too, but I couldn't make out what they were saying. Just pieces of voices the wind brought, and I wondered about why I couldn't see them or hear them when I was on the ground. But somehow, when I got back to the ground, I clean forgot about that.

I loved the trees—especially that one, even before it was a wavy tree. But I loved the smooth rocks, too. There was one by the pond, and, even when it was cold outside, it would let the sun warm it up. I could feel the sunshine if I put my cheek against it.

Like I said, time was funny there. Once, when I was soaking up bits of winter sunshine from the rock, I opened my eyes and realized that it was spring, and it was warm! I could see right down into the pond. Lily pads floated on the top and reflected down and up again, and, when I just let my eyes go and do what they wanted, I couldn't tell how many lily pads I was looking at. And way down, down in the water was something shiny. Like metal. I couldn't tell how deep the pond was because of all the reflecting going on.

The tree became two trees, maybe more. One grow-ing out of the ground I stood on and a sort of wavy one growing out of the ground on the bottom of the pond. The sky was upside-down in the pond. I even checked that out from way up the tree, and I could see another me way down, down the pond. Down in the upside-down, wavy tree.

I wanted to go check that out. It was fine just playing with the trees and the rocks and Little Man, but what fun it would be to have another me to play with! And there was nothing but I was going to find out what that shiny thing was. So I just shimmied down the tree. I took off my clothes and my shoes, and I left them right at the base of the tree. And I told Little Man not to go running off with them, but I reckon he did.

I went down, down into the water. I had to remind myself to open my eyes, because I wanted to see this other wavy world. I kept going down, and I was holding my breath, so I reminded myself to breathe. I gasped in a huge breath of wavy world air. At first it was hard to breathe it, but then got the hang of it, just like shimmying up the tree. And I sort of broke through something, like the very thinnest plate of ice, so thin I hardly noticed it, but I knew I'd broken through because things were no longer wavy. I looked up and saw the wavy world was now where I'd just come from. Funny, huh?

I say, I reckon Little Man took my dress up to the house and gave it to Mama, 'cause I saw her up there holding my dress and crying hard. And Little Man was all wet and barking and splashing in and out of the water. But he wasn't barking loud. I could barely hear him. I really wish she'd stop crying.

And then time seemed to skip around again like it does there. I'd shimmied all the way to the fork in the tree and watched them. The blanket that was just for me was all wrapped around the wavy me in the world that used to be the not wavy place. But I didn't mind. And Little Man was sort of crying, too, the way crazy ol' hound dogs cry, and Pa had dug a big hole right at the base of the wavy tree.

I really do wish they'd stop crying. They need to remember to look up and look down. Then they'd know. Then maybe they'd see the shiny thing, too.

Dewey

An old red and white International Harvester pulling a plow is driven by a hard, young man. He'd been at it since the first rays of sun, and now the humidity is making the man nearly slide off the seat. Oh, wait—there is his wife at the end of the row, God bless her heart. She's got the blue and white thermos jug and he knows it's full of icy lemonade. And she brought a towel, too.

That's a good woman, standing there in her white dress with the little yellow flowers, a tan apron with ruffles all around, and her hair pulled atop her head. Why does she bother ironing those aprons? Why does she bother, when by mid-morning, everything will be as limp and lifeless as a dandelion a child picks for his mother and brings home in his pocket?

Maybe it's because she's got no little ones to keep her mind on more important things than ironing her two ragged aprons. Maybe her father was right when he said, "That boy couldn't harvest a decent crop of corn if the Lord Himself did the planting."

Why on Earth did he marry her? She was so delicate-boned and cheerful. So sweet and, my God, how she loved him. As out of place as her grandmother's fine china tea cup on their plank wood table.

He could have married the girl down the road. Everyone expected him to. She was born to these ways, and they'd have had a decent enough life. She was sturdier-built and, going by her sisters, would have two or three chubby little ones by this time. That girl wouldn't have ironed aprons.

He stopped the tractor a good hundred paces from the end of the row. He climbed down, took off his straw hat and slicked back his sweat-drenched hair as best he could. Then he flung the sweat from his hands and bent to collect a small bouquet of violets growing in the shade of a clump of gypsum.

The delicate flowers in his big, calloused, dirty hand made him smile and as he looked up to catch his wife's eyes. He asked God to slap him hard if he ever passed up a chance to give that girl violets.

Anna

She put on her freshly-ironed apron and made lemon-ade in the blue and white thermos jug. She thought he must be feeling like the rag she'd just used to clean the kitchen floor and wrung out. It was so hot and humid, and sitting on that hot old tractor must be plum hellish. She grabbed a towel for him to dry off a bit and headed to the end of the field he was plowing.

He worked so hard, and she knew she wasn't much help. She wasn't a great cook, like his mama or any of the other women around here for that matter. His mama, who told her to call her Mama B, was kind to her in a way and had taught her, when they were first married, how to kill and dress a chicken. But she knew Mama B laughed about it with the rest of the family. And when she was out of the room for a bit at the church circle, she'd overheard Mama B tell the others, "Bless her heart, that child turned flat out white when she saw that head-less chicken run around in circles! Near fainted, she did."

Then Cora Lee from just down the road said, "Well, that's what happens when you marry a girl who just isn't cut out for it," and that was the end of the laughter and that conversation.

She knew everyone had expected her husband to marry Cora Lee's middle daughter. That girl was strong. She would probably have the whole house spotless by sunrise, stack bales in the afternoon, and birth a baby boy in the evening right after washing up from a huge supper. "But there is no way she could love him like I do," she said outloud. "Love's gotta count for something."

She waited at the end of the row. The tractor shimmered in the heat. She wondered how there could be so much dust on such a steamy day. She watched him as he stopped the tractor well off from her and bent to get something off the ground. She smoothed her apron and fixed a loose strand of hair and wondered if Cora Lee's daughter could feel this sort of sweet electricity just watching her husband of over two years walk toward her, all covered in dirt and sweat.

She Ate the Ice Cream

She finally realized that no one could possibly understand what she was feeling.

No one.

Her friends were tiring of her increasing darkness nearly as much as she was. She knew that. She saw them very seldom any more. She disconnected her phone. She was very lonely and wanted to see no one.

The medications didn't help. Therapy was ridiculous. Even the electroshock that was "guaranteed" to work only seemed to make the darkness deeper and heavier for her to carry. A psychologist told her she had a high IQ and a personality disorder. Very convenient diagnoses that meant "hopeless."

Her Buddhist friends told her to let it flow through her. A priest told her to pray the Rosary daily. A pastor prayed with her and congregations prayed for her. Another sort of priest even exorcised some demons out of her. A monk told her to not mind it, that the depression didn't exist.

But it was impossible to let a concrete wall flow through her. She had been praying daily for as long as she could remember. The banished demons didn't seem to have been the cause of the darkness, and it was impossible for her not to mind her mind in this condition.

A trainer told her to eat only fruits, vegetables, whole grains and beans, drink only water, and run through the pain. She did that until a neighbor found her lying flat on her face in the middle of the street in her running clothes and helped her home. Now she tried to remember the last time she ate anything.

More than a few people told her that everyone has down days and that she needed to put on her big girl panties and get over it. More than a few people told her flat out that she didn't want to get better—that she used depression as an excuse.

An excuse for what, she didn't know. She couldn't imagine how she profited from this. But she understood how frustrated people were with her. She was more frustrated than anyone. Frustrated and exhausted and depleted and without hope.

There was no decision left. It was the easiest thing—it was the only easy thing she could remember doing.

She ate the ice cream that a friend had brought her a month or so earlier. It had been in the freezer so long it had crystals on the top, and she had to let it thaw a bit before she could eat it. She realized that most people would find the ice cream delicious and comforting. She couldn't taste it, but she found it very comforting.

Then she took her pills. She took the current prescriptions first, emptying the bottles. She started to feel a bit good. Then she took the older prescriptions—the ones that doctors had discontinued. She felt hopeful. She found the over-the-counter pain relievers, the left over cold medicine, and an unopened box of crackers. She took them and three glasses of water to her bedroom, found an old movie on TV and had a picnic on her bed.

She felt a little nauseated, but mostly she felt relaxed, very sleepy. She noticed that she physically couldn't open her eyes or move her mouth, but she felt as if she were smiling. Really, truly smiling for the first time in her life.

And she saw an impossibly intense pinpoint of blue light. So beautiful. It came toward her. Slowly or quickly, she couldn't tell. No, it was she moving toward the light. Maybe. It no longer mattered. It could have been an eternity; it could have been a nanosecond. It could have been.

It could have been.

Quilt

See this old patchwork quilt?
So my old granny said
Her ma sewed every stitch
For my granny's bed.

Cut from flour sacks,
Scraps from sewing clothes,
Each patch tells its own tale,
And so our story grows.

It kept my granny warm
On cold, snowy nights.
Three sisters in a bed,
Bundled up so tight.

This quilt kept them both dry,
The day Dad married Mom.
It covered both their heads
In a cold, wet storm.

As it dried before the fire,
They let the cold wind blow.
Safe within their home
They made our story grow.

I'll proudly make our bed,
When I find my bride.
'Neath this old patchwork quilt,
She'll lay right by my side.

And if the good Lord wills
What we want the most,
Our love will bring new life
And let our story grow.

SECTION III

Au Naturel

Bigger than That

You can tell me there is no God,
And I'll tell you a story.
You can show me scientific proof,
And I'll show you an oak tree.

You can tell me that Noah stuffed his boat
    with every species,
And I'll show you dinosaur bones.
You can tell me that prayers are unheard,
And I'll show you a starry summer night on the prairie.

I swim in answered prayers and breathe miracles.

Wake up and look around you.
Open your mind and your eyes.
Listen to your soul.
God is the whole.

We are not doomed.
We are not accidental.
We are all blessed beyond all reason.
We are given teachers. We are given guides.

The soup needs no more ingredients.
So, call God by whatever name you will.
God is beyond all names.
God is bigger than that.

Middle-Aged Maple Leaf

I asked for a dream that would help me, and I dreamed of a colorful maple leaf floating on a still lake.

My friend said the maple leaf has no ability to manipulate its path or change its destination. He said it's controlled by the flow of the lake and will eventually be washed onto shore and left, as the water continues on its path.

I'm glad it wasn't his dream.

I think the beautiful maple leaf was at the end of her season on the tree. Once a yellow-green bud, she'd grown into a large green leaf—one of hundreds of thousands. She worked hard with photosynthesis, providing shade for what was below, providing protection for bird, squirrel, and beings she didn't even know. She often provided a meal for a small worm or two. She turned her face to greet the sun each day. Then, over the course of a few days, she turned red and yellow and shimmered in the autumn sun.

One day, she just let go. She floated gently down and landed on the silver lake beneath her branch. She enjoyed being held and gently rocked there. It was a new season, though a shorter one.

She became a raft for dragonfly faeries and a nursery for water insects, and a model for a photographer. The water grew colder, and it pulled her down where she lay on the sand and rocks under the water.

There, she completed releasing her energy. She was no longer leaf. It was another new season. She became snail, fertile mud, insect, fish, oxygen, nitrogen, and the cycle continued.

Ocean

Rise and fall, rise and fall.
Stretching, reaching tall above.
Reaching up for her, Moon, his love.
Rise and fall, rise and fall.

Sometimes destructive,
Smashing rock with rage released.
Sometimes sparkling,
Melting rock-hard hearts with peace.

Rise and fall, rise and fall.
Everything beneath his Moon
Does follow suit,
Longing for a deep kiss soon.

Such Big Love

I will be the Mother's ears
    and love each word you say,
I will be the Mother's pain
    and take all yours away,
I will be the Mother's eyes
    and show you what is true,
I will be the Mother's arms
    and gently cradle you.

I will be the Mother's light
    and walk you down your road,
And if you ever falter,
    I will lighten up your load,
And when you have confusion,
    I will calm your every fear,
And you will ever always know
    your Mother Earth is near.

Such big Love,
    Bigger than the sea,
Such big Love,
    To know Her is to be,

Au Naturel

Such big Love,
    All Nature and all Earth
Such big Love,
    Has given us new birth.

I will be the Mother's voice
    and sing your lullaby,
Mother's tears will fall like rain
    if every you should cry,
The Mother's smile will shine on you
    with every waking day,
And I will be the Mother's ears
    and love every word you say.

When I Knew

When I was a child, I rested my chin on a smooth, flat stone, warmed by the sun, and I became part of the tall grass song.

I was held in the strong arms of the maple trees, and the leaves taught me how to turn my face to the sun.

I ate cherries, apples, pears, rhubarb, plums, grapes washed only by the rain. And the fruit and the rain and I were the same.

I lay flat on my back in the grass and watched the stars and the fireflies, and I began to glow and twinkle.

Eagles taught me to soar over the river by joining unseen thermals.

Beneath the skirt of the tall spruce tree I sat on a carpet of flat brown needles during a gentle rain, and I became the smell of pine.

I buried my face in lilacs—purple, violet, white—and learned to giggle with their soft power.

I sat hugging my knees in an open field in rain that stung, while green and white lightning pulled at my skin and thunder shook my chest.

And then I knew I am.

Autumn Moon

She,

round, ripe,

orangeyellowgold,

beautiful and shy,

hides behind the black lace

of trees.

Dance

I danced with an oak leaf today.
She, not new-green-sprouting,
Was crisp-brown-delicate.
She'd hung on to the branch all winter
And chose today to let go,
Defying gravity just two seconds more,
To dance with me!

Dusk

Dusk paints with a steady brush.
She doesn't dawdle, doesn't rush.
She changes colors with her whim,
From sky to treetops closing in.

Shadows grow so long and tall,
Until, it seems, they cover all,
Encouraging shy stars to glow,
Blessing all who watch below.

Flow

My energy vibrates with the chair,
    the deck, the ground,
        the planet;

All exchanging energy and matter.

And the only boundaries between
    my nose and the crescent moon
        are those I imagine.

Go figure.

We are all We—
    One Universe—
        All Divine.

I am the oak tree that looks like dark lace.
    I am the blue/gray/yellow sky.
        I am the stars, the dust of which
           we are all made.

I'm Already Here

My death becomes my marriage with the Earth,
My lover and provider since my birth.
See me in my wedding gown of dewy spring green
    leaves,
And a million stars will dance with me
     above the summer breeze.

Celebrate my wedding with me, friends!
With every grand beginning something ends.
See me learning how to fly when Autumn twirls the dry
    leaves by,
And Winter writes my poems on glass again.

If a crow calls something out to you,
You will know inside you that it's true.
I will be that message, or if the mountains want to
    share
A secret with you, you'll know I am there.

In the river ever-changing and the same,
Across the meadow you may hear your name.
The silver liquid moonlight and the buttery warm sun,
Will breathe for me when my breath is done.

So, you see, no mourning is required,
A new adventure takes me ever higher.
There is no such thing as death,
Nothing left to fear.
I won't return to Earth, my friends,
I'm already here.

Testosterone

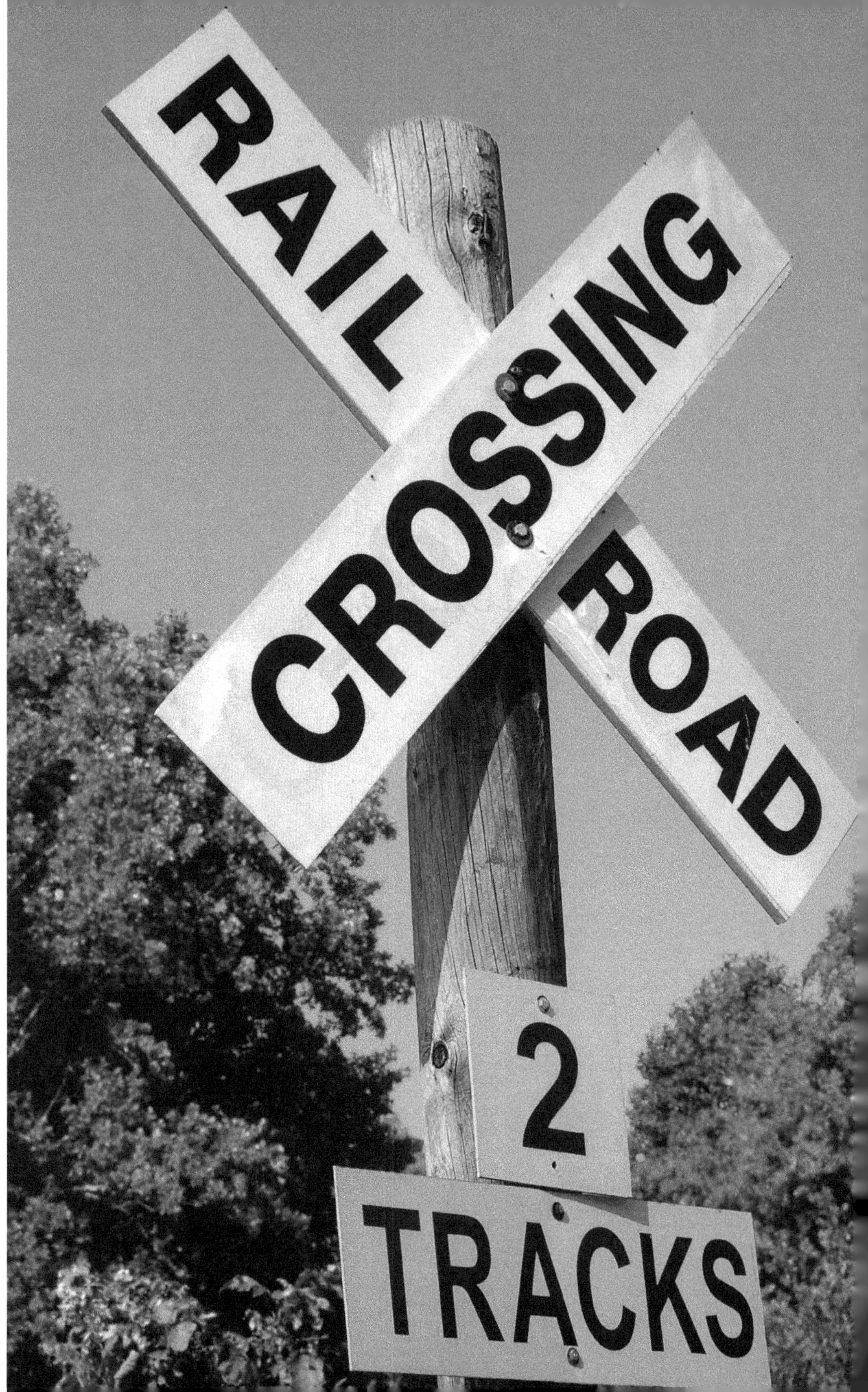
RAIL
ROAD
CROSSING
2
TRACKS

Freight Train

He spread his coat on the gravel pile,
Not comfortable, but the boy had style.
And all the while, just feet away,
Roared a freight train.

It was a long,
    slow
        train.

And afterward, through pouring rain,
We ran to his house along the tracks,
And made love again,
    And again,
        For no other reason than
            Because we could.

As light and inconsequential
It seemed from the start,
I must admit
    He broke my heart,
        Probably for no other reason than
        Because he could.

Golden Potentialities

He was my first.
And living as we did on neighboring small islands
In oceans of corn and soybean fields,
We found a tractor path.

It was summer, and there was no light,
    except the moon
And millions of stars.
And we were awkward,
    powered by his hormones, my love,
And millions of stars.

And afterward, silently,
We walked hand in hand down the path,
Surrounded by corn just tasseling,
Not knowing the appropriate thing to say.

My love grew as fast as the corn that summer,
And we became less awkward,
And we made up things to say.
And the ears showed silver silk.

The corn hardened and turned to gold.
The leaves turned into brown paper
That rustled in the breeze and crumbled in the rain.
And still, there were the stars, always in my eyes,
    keeping me from seeing.

But I went away to school,
And there were too many lights to see the stars,
And he found out that one girl
Is pretty much as good as another.

During our last conversation on the phone,
I told him a white lie.
With relief he said,
"You know, that would have ruined my life."

I couldn't cry.
But now I cry once a year in late May.
I pick a wild flower and toss it into a readied field
Full of golden potentialities.

Nontraditional Student

*H*e was twenty-six or so—a nontraditional student. I was eighteen or so—nontraditional in a different way. He was lead in a play in which I had a walk-on. I liked the leads, the leaders, the standouts.

Well, really, who doesn't?

He offered me a ride home from the party after the show closed. We stopped at his house for a glass of wine, which sounded quite grown-up to me. We drank some cheap wine out of jelly glasses.

We had "a glass of wine" now and then for a semester or so. Then one day he said, "I think I represent a father figure to you."

I said, "That's the stupidest thing I've ever heard," and threw him out with a great, dramatic slamming of the screen door.

Unfortunately, it was his house.

He left anyway, late for a rehearsal or something, and I walked home.

Zeke

A puff of smoke, a gentle breeze,
Can't hold them in my hand,
Sparkling stars on summer seas,
Writing in the sand.

If I could make this world anew,
I would include them all.
And I'd include our brief affair—
The ride was worth the fall.

The Next Door

She was retired today. She went in to the office as she'd done for the past four and a half decades and was greeted by the director. He said something about appreciating her years of service to the company, the hard work and selfless overtime she'd put in, and that she now "deserved" to be retired.

That's the word he used. *Deserved.*

The personal items she had in her office all fit in one small box. That seemed a bit funny to her. This job had consumed all of her—or rather, she willingly gave all of herself to this job. She felt as if all she had left were the narrow margins of life.

She lived alone in the same small apartment she'd occupied for 45 years. She hadn't even noticed when the neighborhood changed. The building looked bedraggled now, and the grocery down the street had bars over the windows.

She looked around her apartment. Had she never noticed that the walls were drab and colorless? Her office was a sunny yellow, and the desk set bright orange. She started to take a frozen dinner out and stopped.

"Screw this," she said out loud. And then a bit louder, "No! FUCK this!" She had never uttered that word before, and she was a bit scared by how good it felt. She stuffed the TV dinner back in the freezer and got in her car and drove.

Having no destination in mind, she didn't realize how long it might take to get there. She stopped at a neighborhood pub. Not her neighborhood. Not her pub. She went in and sat at the bar and ordered a glass of red wine.

"No. Wait. Make that a martini."

She noticed the bartender's smile. He smiled with his whole face. He looked like a truly happy person might look, she thought.

He set the drink down in front of her and asked, "New to the neighborhood? I don't remember seeing you here before."

"Oh, no, no. I'm not from this neighborhood. I'm from Damion Kline," she said before she realized that her former employer wasn't actually a neighborhood. "I mean, that is, I used to be. I mean ..." She sipped the martini and wondered how in the world anyone could actually enjoy the taste of them.

"I mean I was retired today." She stirred the cold drink with the skewer of olives. "And I just realized that I forgot something."

"What did you forget?" the young man asked.

"I forgot to have a life."

He started to laugh and realized she was serious. Here she was, what? Must be mid-sixties at least. She wasn't bad-looking for someone old enough to be his mother, he thought. And she didn't seem sad as much as she seemed just lost.

She found herself talking to the chestnut-haired bartender as if she'd known him for years. She even laughed a little. She hadn't realized that she'd finished the martini when he put another one in front of her.

"Ok, Max. See you tomorrow," he called to a man just leaving.

She looked around and realized that she was now the only customer in the pub, and the young man was locking the front door.

"Oh, I'm sorry. I'm keeping you from going home," she said and started to gather herself from the bar stool. She found the floor had become oddly unstable.

"Hold on, now," he said and helped her back to her seat. "You aren't keeping me from anything. Besides, this is my home."

She found herself laughing at that. "I sure know that feeling!"

"No," he said, chuckling a bit, "I mean I live upstairs." He was now sitting next to her, and he very slowly turned her bar stool to face him. "What is your name?"

His eyes were so brown and soft, "Like mink," she thought. "Margaret."

"I'm Jamie," he said, taking her face so gently in his hands. "And I think it's never too late to remember to have a life. All you have to do is go through the next door."

The next morning, very early, she left the note on his dresser. The little notepad in her purse said, "From the Desk of Margaret" across the top. She crossed out Desk and wrote Life.

> *Dear Jamie,*
> *Thank you for showing me the door.*
>
> *Margaret*

Sax Man

No one ever told me there were men like you.
  I never read a book that told me what to do
When the music from the saxophone
  Won't leave your melting heart alone,
And cuts from fifty jagged words are healed
    With only two:
      For you.

Play me something, Sax Man,
  Play me something sweet.
Surrounded by the sound,
  I feel almost complete.
I just let go, let too much show.
    I know, I know, I know you know.
      So play it low.

Do it to me Sax Man,
  Play me one more time.
Let this mouth of mine now be your reed.

Do it to me Sax Man,
  Play me smooth and slow.
I promise you that I'll be every key you need.

Naked Me

Is it the brass or my skin
    Your skilled fingers bless?
Is it the music or your breath I feel my neck caress?

Help me, man, I'm falling,
    And I can't find the floor.
Your music—our music—keeps me wanting more.

No one ever told me there were men like you.
    But now I could write a book about just what to do
When the music from the saxophone
    Won't leave your melting heart alone,
And cuts from fifty jagged words are healed
      With only two:
        For you.

        For you.

Not Quite Perfect

I made a mental list of everything I wanted in a man.

Intelligence. That had to be number one.

Educated. Well, that would do in place of some intelligence, but certainly not all. Intelligence *and* education preferred.

Open Mind.

Talent. A must.

Wit. If he can't keep up, forget it.

Not making the list were money, a good head of hair, and classic good looks. Unfortunately, in the list, I forgot to include Nice.

So, when I met him, I thought, well maybe. Ph.D., old hippy rocker who could play guitar well enough to sing along, and witty enough to make up songs on the spur of the moment.

But then came sex, and all bets were off! This man had the most perfect penis I've ever seen. Not the longest, not the thickest, but perfectly shaped, with a big, round, happy face, not dissimilar to the knob on the end of a stick shift in a very hot classic car. And he knew what to do with it.

I remember other things about him, too. I remember making out in pubs, without a care who was watching. I remember his knowledge of women's sexuality was down-right dangerous. I remember checking the ceiling in the morning for signs of scratch marks. I know that he enjoyed our adventures at least as much as I did, and he promised me—*promised me*—that there would never be a time when we'd have to give them up. That man seriously spun my head around.

He said, "I love you, I love you, I love you," while making love. "Let's go to Mexico or Alaska. Just you and me, and we'll get by."

Of course, he never said these things when we weren't having sex, and we never had sex without being severely under the influence. I wonder, Jose Quervo, are you really a friend of mine?

Not My Friend

This man is not my friend.
So if you see me lost in his brown eyes,
Or if he sneaks and hugs me by surprise,
If he holds me when we dance,
Or if his smile speaks of romance,
If I start to think there is a chance,
There is something you must do.

Put me on the train to Chicago,
Or strand me in Key Largo.
If you have to, put me on a plane to France!
Drag me to Massachusetts,
I don't care, even Los Cruses.
Just don't let me get into that devil's pants!

This man is not my friend.
So, if you see my mind remembering the passion,
If you care for me, you'll give my head a bashin'.
If his touch lingers too long,
You know I can't be that strong.
Even if I say, "I don't care that it's wrong,"
There's something I'd like you to do.

Naked Me

Get me outta there that minute.
Don't you dare leave me there in it.
If you have to, you can hit me on the head!
I'm addicted to him, you see.
One more withdrawal will kill me.
So you cannot let me take that man to bed!

This man is not my friend.
But sometimes we pretend.
Because in bed we really light up the whole sky.

So, though he's not my friend,
He has the power to send
Me to the moon!
The fall back is when I pay.
There must be a better way,
And I really hope I find it very soon!

Lake House

It's been a minor curse that I fall in love with assholes, and a major curse that I've often been one.

I met a man with sand-colored hair and hazel eyes. He pursued me. When we first met, he told me he was "almost divorced." I told him I was allergic to men who were almost divorced. I told him to go have a transition woman and then call me.

Damned if he didn't do just that several months later.

He was pretty much a dream man—tall, gorgeous, sexy, rich. But he loved me too much, and I was greatly cursed.

We spent weeks at his perfect vacation house on a crystal clear lake in the woods.

One perfect day, I looked at him and cried because I knew what was coming. Men like that should not love women like me.

I Know, I Know

I know, I know,
But even so ...
You don't have to say it again,
Just let it go.

Ah, you and I,
We come and we go.
That's how it's always been,
I know, I know.

I held you in my heart;
I held you in my soul.
There's nothing left of me to hold to,
No place left to go.

You say you can't hold me now;
I just need to feel.
I know it's over now,
And I'm keeping it real.

TESTOSTERONE

You say you've found someone
With guidance from above.
What does that make me, my friend?
What does that make our love?

Don't bother. I know.

Blow My Mind

If you've had a chance to change your mind,
I don't mind to wait in line,
Cause what you've got's so very fine.
Darlin' you just blow my mind!

Well I don't need to make you mine,
And I'm not sayin' for all time,
But I think it would be a crime
To miss it while we're in our prime.

So give me just a little sign,
And, Baby, I'll turn on a dime,
And I will always have the time,
'Cause I love the way our fun lines rhyme.

I reckon it's about sublime.
And I ain't religious most the time,
But what you do's about divine.
So come on, Darlin', blow my mind!

Thinkin' 'bout That Man

I've been thinkin' 'bout that man.
It was, oh, so long ago.
Now and then, if the tune is just right
And my man's outta sight,
I just can't help but let it go.

Lord, I been thinkin' 'bout that man
And how—every single day—
How he made me laugh or made me cry,
Lord, it didn't matter why,
Tears were never far away.

Friends used to ask me why
I'd just follow stage to stage.
Didn't seem to have my own—
Just one line upon his page.

But I didn't hear their words,
Cause I was happy as a song.
And I never missed a chance,
Though I was only just along.

NAKED ME

But, when I think about that man
And the night he sang for me,
That ol' feeling's back again.
And my heart remembers when
His music set me free.

Gone as I Can Be

You said you'd always love me
Until the day you die,
And I would always answer
With an oh-so-solemn sigh.

You said you'd always need me—
Without me you'd be blue.
You said I really send you,
And I said you send me, too.

You send me, Baby,
And I'm just as gone as I can be.
You really sent me.
I'm just as gone as I can be.

Then just last night you called me,
And said you must be true.
You said you'd found an other,
And you worried what I'd do.

Well, yes, it's true I wanted you,
And we had lots of fun,
But, I guess that I should tell you now,
You weren't the only one.

Naked Me

You feared there was no fury
Like a woman scorned.
You feared that I just sit around
And do no more than mourn.

I ain't chasin', I ain't cryin',
I won't sit around and whine,
Cause when it comes to missing you
I haven't got the time.

Don't tell me good-bye,
I'm just as gone as I can be.
Don't worry, Baby,
I'm just as gone as I can be.

Death of a Secret

To whom can I confess a sin I don't regret?
When all that seems to matter is a secret too long kept?
It's all very well and good to say I must move on;
Will there be nothing left of us, now that you're gone?

We tucked our joys and tears in the pockets of our
    souls
To bring along and share in the hours that we stole.
Do you remember how exciting it all was from the
    start?
The rareness, the adventure, the racing of our hearts?

It kept us young, you said, and I agreed.
No need to wreck our lives to feed a lovers' greed.
I shared our memories with only you
(Well, with secrets, that's what you have to do).

No albums filled with photos of family holidays,
Just those printed in my memory, and someday those
    will haze.
I can't even share my mourning, friends don't under-
    stand my tears
What will I do without you in my remaining years?

Required Happiness

She closed her eyes and saw him as she'd seen him that night. Her dark-eyed friend had leaned against his little sports car after driving thirteen hours to wish her happy birthday.

"Are you happy?" he had asked.

Well, what was she supposed to say? The Professor had given her this extraordinary party. All her family, all their friends were dancing to the band on the deck, eating, drinking. Of course she was happy right then. It was required to be happy right then.

He said he was going to find a place to sleep and get up early and drive back home. She so wanted him to ask her again in a month or maybe two months. She wanted him to see through her smile and listen to her good-bye kiss.

Oh, but timing never was their strong suit. Sometimes she thought they had everything a good relationship should have, except timing. And that really was everything, wasn't it?

Two months following the party, the Professor had demanded as much from her as she was willing to give to him, and she moved into a tiny apartment.

She called her dark-eyed friend, and he told her he'd taken up with his ex-wife. She had to chuckle. Even 700 miles away his voice carried a sort of required happiness.

Over the years they both tried to glue broken hearts

together with instant love and not to break any more.

Required happiness is happiness after all. It is a shot of anesthesia that makes one's broken heart go numb. She thought it might feel very much like healing, though now she realized she'd never actually experienced healing. It had to be better, she thought, than just feeling the pain.

Love Song to Leonard Cohen*

Look at me, Leonard, when I'm naked in my way,
Not for one last time, with filmed vision every day.
Look upon me tenderly and look upon me long,
And you'll know that I'm half crazy just because of a
   few songs.
You hurt me with democracy
And your silky-smooth, soft honesty.

(Using lint the gaps to fill in
From Buddha, Christ or Dylan
Mix it in with innate wisdom
You don't even know you own)

But it's ok and it is righteous
You are speaking to the rest of us
Your eyes and voice I feel so very deep.

And I'll love you by the river, in the water and the reeds
Until we're both swept under by the passion of our
   deeds.
Some holy dove above us moves.
What water isn't holy, too?

TESTOSTERONE

And all the breaths we'll breathe are now so few.
I'm sorry that we didn't meet 'fore my youth and beauty
fleeted.

I'm nothing if not a muse you never needed.

*One needs to be familiar with the lyrics of
Leonard Cohen to get the most juice out of this piece.

The Last Word

You always had to get the last word in,
    didn't you?
You have to prove yourself right,
Because, maybe, you were wrong before?
    Is that it?

You said you knew I loved you,
    And you said you loved me,
        And I knew it was the truth.

And we loved across the miles,
But you've got to admit, we loved best in each other's
    arms,
Even though you said the distance wouldn't matter
    with our love, based in the ethers as it was.

And I've got to admit, love grows and glows in the
    ethers.
Your blue eyes always saved their sadness, even when
    you proved your joy.
I loved you from the center of me. Why couldn't that
    have been enough to keep you here?

Testosterone

You said you were dying.
I said we all are.
I accused you of focusing on death and avoiding life.
I said don't talk about it.
And the center of me dimmed a bit.
And what did you do?

You died.

You always had to get the last word in,
     didn't you?
Did it have to be good-bye?

About the Author

*F*ay Campbell was raised and raised her children in rural Illinois. She obtained a BA and MSEd from Western Illinois University. She has lived in a variety of areas and environments from Chicago's North Side to a cabin on a ridge in Appalachia. She enjoys gardening, though she's not very good at it, photography, and spending time with her ever expanding, groovy family.

Enamored with exploring the Earth, Fay has traveled much of the U.S. and has visited Australia, England, and China, appreciating Nature.

www.FayCampbell.com

CAMPIAN BELLSTONE PUBLISHERS
Richmond, Virginia

www.BellstoneBooks.com